Dr. Henrietta Abeley Abbey

Copyright © 2023 by Dr. Henrietta A. Abbey

All right reserved

No part of this book may be reproduced, or stored in retrieval system, or transmitted in any form of by any means, electronics, mechanical, photocopying, recording, or otherwise, without express written permission of the author.

Cover design by: US BOOK PRESS Printed in the

United States of America

This genre is dedicated to all deceased professors and supporting staffs of Walden University. Also, to all late students and alumni of Walden Community.
My sincere silence to those that fell during the COVID era.

Dr. Henrietta Abeley Abbey

Finance and Budget Sampling of a Comparative Council: Finance & Budget Analysis of the New York City Police Department

Project completed on February 6th, 2016

Table of Contents

Abstract 6
Introduction 7
A gist background of New York City Police
Department and the mission statements 8
Ethical considerations related to finance
and budgeting within the NYPD 10
Technological considerations for improving
the efficiency of finance and
budgeting in the NYPD 12
Applicable laws, regulations and
policies affecting the NYPD financial and
budgetary operations 16
Evaluation of the NYPD budget process
and revenue sources Budget Cycle 18
Internal factors impacting successful
strategic financial planning 22
The NYPD's usage of cost-benefit analysis 23
Evaluation of the NYPD's
annual financial report 25
Assessment of the NYPD's
overall financial condition 29
Conclusion 31
References 32
The Language of Leadership: 34
Abstract 35
Introduction 36
Bloomberg's biography 38

Bloomberg's contribution to
society and New York City *39*
Leadership Analysis *42*
Leadership Recommendations *45*
Conclusions *49*
References *50*
Abstract *53*
Introduction *54*
Social Change as a social issue *55*
Learned topic on social change as a research problem *56*
Description of a research gap in my study *57*
The gap that the study will address *58*
From the gap, create a brief purpose statement
 that is aligned with the following research question:
What is the meaning of social change for
Walden graduate students? *59*
The role of the researcher *60*
Data Sources of social change *62*
Instrumentation of data *63*
Data Analysis *65*
Coding of data *66*
Chart *68*
Trustworthiness *69*
Summary *71*
References *72*

Abstract

This project is about the New York City Police Department, the mission, and an in-depth analysis of its finance and budgeting. Subjects in the analysis include; evaluation of internal key points affecting strategic planning, the department's cost-benefit data, assessment of the annual financial information, and the current financial status of the department.

Introduction

In modern world financial planning activities are commonly seen in families, organizations, institutions, and establishments. During planning, planners take into consideration funds available, and calculate the expenditures within the means and capacity of resources and revenue available. Government agencies obtain funds from federal coffers and tax payer's account. Since the public pay taxes and such funds are used in maintaining government organizations, infrastructures, bridges, roads, streets, tunnels, parks, public buildings, and recreational amenities, the public are supposed to know what the funds are used for, and how it is used. So, in most of the government agencies, every fiscal year, they release and publicize the fiscal finance and budgeting for the coming year to the press in order for the public to be aware of monetary analysis of the coming year. Not only do they state the fiscal year data but also include an estimate for subsequent years. An example of government agency that experiences finance and budgeting procedures is the New York Police Department.

A gist background of New York City Police Department and the mission statements

The New York City Police Department (NYPD) was discovered in 1845 (New York City Police Department, n.d.). It serves the five boroughs of New York City, which are: Brooklyn, Bronx, Manhattan, Queens and Staten Island. The primary duties of the NYPD are law enforcement and investigation in New York City. The NYPD was the first Police Department established in America (New York Police Department, n.d.). The current commissioner for the NYPD is Police Commissioner William Bill Bratton who was elected by Mayor Bill De Blasio on January 1st, 2014.

There are several branches in the NYPD such as the Emergency Service Unit, Canine Unit, Air Support Unit, Bomb Squad, Counter-Terrorism, Intelligence Division, Anti-Gang Unit, Anti-Organized Crime Unit, Narcotics Unit, Public Transportation Unit, Public Housing Police Division, Transit Police Division, the Auxiliary Police Offices Unit, Traffic Division and lastly School Safety Division (New York City Police Department, n.d.). The NYPD has seventy-seven Precincts, twelve Transit Districts, and nine Housing Police Services (New York City Police Department, n.d.). The Police Department has approximately 8,839 Police cars, eleven boats, eight helicopters, one hundred and twenty horses, thirty-one German shepherd dogs and three bloodhound's dogs (New York City Police Department, n.d.).

The mission and vision of the NYPD is: to promote, enhance, and replenish curtesy, professionalism, and respect among employees and the general public; to serve the public in the best of its ability, and to aide in building solid rapport in the communities, and among neighbors, and to assist in fighting terrorism activities. Also the department envisions to bring communities together by holding community coalitions in the commands and jurisdiction of the Police Department, and to ensure safety for all people by dispatching Police Officers to patrol streets and surroundings of New York City. The department issues summons to drivers who don't abide by traffic rules, and regulations of the Department of Motor Vehicle, and they ensure the proper use of streets, roads, highways, and parking meters. Lastly, the department wants to promote quality of life through the operations of the 311 system whereby the general public could call to make complaints about noise, smoking in restricted public areas, dog leashing, dog curbing, neighbor's wellness and general wellness check, illegal parking, blocked driveway, and for the purpose of reporting non-criminal activities which are threats to health, the public and neighbors.

Ethical considerations related to finance and budgeting within the NYPD

The organization is funded by tax payer's money, federal, state, city funds, and revenue generated by Police issuing tickets, fines, arrests and summons. Decisions for the spending in the department are made up of the mayor, the police commissioner, some stakeholders, and other city agency personnel. Sometimes, the department has to cut down on its expenses when allotted limited funds. This means that certain programs offered by the department would not be available when funds are less. For instance, supervisors were supposed to go for additional training in 2015 but lack of extra revenue made it impossible for the training program to go on. Therefore the supervisors did not receive additional training in 2015 as anticipated, and that was a blow, and disappointment for some workers who looked forward to attending such programs. Although unknown, the effect of the canceled training could affect employees' performances and evaluations thereby affecting effective productivity (Bryson, 2011).

It is hard to budget with limited funds and resources however; the department manages with the funds received from the government. Some priority spending in the department includes wages, over-time for police officers, training for the officers, and celebration of special calendar events. In lieu with sticking to a restricted budget, civilians in the department are not encouraged to do over-time unless necessary. Mostly such civilians are asked to receive hours as over-time instead of cash. In this case, such over-time in hours are accumulated into days whereby the worker could use them at a later time.

The only time civilians get over-time is when they work holidays, and are paid time and a half by law, and do receive an extra day off automatically. These decisions were made by benevolent associations and unions that represent the uniform and civilian workers of the Police Department. Normally before, the unions propose such incentive; they would have conducted background check of the finances of the department to ensure that the department is capable of awarding funds to employees who fall into that category. Therefore over-time during the holidays are legitimate operations that the department can afford civilians aside the hourly over-times.

The NYPD is part of a city agency that caters for public safety and quality of life in New York City. In a scenario, the government agencies can be described as the total human being with several parts that function to coordinate movement and function as a person. Each government agency has its own functioning in government. For instance the office of Management and Budget is the government agency that starts preparing the budget from October for the next coming year expenditures. The Office of Comptroller is the agency that distributes government funds to city agencies. The fiscal year starts on July 1, of the New Year, and funds are released to the various city agencies. The Council of the City of New York function is to publish the budget information via media so that the public and the agencies can have access to new planned budgets.

Technological considerations for improving the efficiency of finance and budgeting in the NYPD

Currently, the NYPD uses Intranet for all computer operations. It also uses LAN and WAN soft-wares. The computers are designed for NYPD purposes only. However the workers can have access to internet, browse for locations, addresses of companies, and search for additional information to complete a report or give direction to the public. However workers can't use the computers for personal access such as Facebook, Twitter, MSN Outlook mails and other emails. Never the less, workers have access to MSN Official homepage. This is because, the land-lines can't harbor all email connections by the workers so access to emails have been blocked. Workers have to use other computer sources to access emails such as phones, tablets and IPad. However, the NYPD has its own Outlook email connections designed specifically for work use only. Employees would not want to use department email page for personal operations because other workers can have access to such messages, and may be a problem. Also the NYPD uses office automated machines such as scanners, shredders, copiers and fax machines. Most of the NYPD's products are manufactured by Dell Computers and Konica Companies. When the computer is dysfunctional, the IT Center dispatches technicians to the commands to fix the problem. Such workers are required to have experience in WAN or LAN, and must be a computer literate. When the copier is broken, Konica Company dispatches a technician to fix the problem. Gone were the days when the NYPD used manual operating machines such as manual typewriter for work.

The department has evolved, and endeavored to grow, and embrace technology to be efficient. It is known that technology replaces manpower, and it is one of the faster's means of work. Since incorporating advanced technology to the department's resources, the NYPD is able to plan successfully in finances because machinery work's faster, and makes fewer mistakes than manual man-power. It is a guarantee that figures are accurately and precisely calculated in the finance department; thanks to computer and advance technology.

So the NYPD has adequate technology in the millennium to improve its finance and budgeting operations. For instance the civilians have ample access to computer so it is a suggestion that the IT Center will design a video program that the supervisors can watch every quarterly, and fill out an assessment questionnaire to assess progress in their various commands. For instance, drivers who are careless, have the opportunity to do an on-line course for defensive driving, and acquire certificate upon completion which they give out to the insurance companies to reduce insurance premiums. The Police Department can design video and internet tutorials, and coaching to civilian supervisors and this will save travelling cost, and additional training expenses at the Police Academy. Such attempts could bring in surplus in the budget to make room for additional resources, and more computers (Mikesell, 2014).

Some technological solutions I recommend that the NYPD incorporate into their system of operation is the effective use of the newly designed cameras on patrol vehicles, snap-shops (body cameras) that can take vivid pictures of incidents that occur. Sometimes the pictures taken are so blurred and dark, and due to such factors sometimes the officers arrest the wrong perpetrators. Victims who are wrongly arrested, and sent to jail for years before discoveries are made of their innocence sue the city for millions of dollars which the Police Department can prevent; if only the cameras available take accurate, clean and clear pictures of the perpetrators. This would help in calculating expenses effectively, and funds needed for certain expenditures don't have to be used for mistakes covered by an electronic device. Although the city pays for these lawsuits at the end of the year, the funds allotted to the department are slashed due to millions of cash used in settling lawsuits against the city agencies. For instance according to Calvi, in 2010, the department paid nearly $1 billion dollars to settle lawsuits. The department feels the pinch because it limits what the department could do for the year.

Also with the changing of passwords for the computers, workers have to call the IT Center, and sometimes there is leak of password, and a compromise of information. The IT Center must design a new technique whereby the workers can change their password frequently on computer not necessarily calling the IT Center. Information received from the public is supposed to be confidential and sometimes when workers use the same password for a longer time, it gets compromise, and others have access to information they not supposed to. A complainant can sue the Police Department for leak of confidentiality which is waste of city funds that could be used wisely in infrastructure or other avenues. According to Byers, technology is modern energy that goes beyond what human energy cannot see (Laureate Education, 2008e). For instance, when the budgeting is done through computerized system, the computer system can alert personnel when password is compromised, or who attempted to use a workers password. Also it monitors revenues, forecasts and assess how revenue is used wisely. Therefore, quality technologies could save the department lots of money, and help in using funds wisely.

Furthermore, the NYPD is in need of constant upgrading of its computer systems as each year new technology advances aligned with new operations. This must be incorporated into finance and budgeting, and funds must be allotted for such upgrades. Also, each year workers must go through training to learn about new designs and developments of upgrades incorporated into the system.

Also constant video tutorials may help workers if there is no money for training, at least workers should have access to video training on their computers to learn of the upgrades. The NYPD, the American Society for Public Administration (ASPA) and the International City/County Management Association (ICMA) must designed advance ethical codes specifically for computer system of operation and the violation terms of its compromise to be abreast with modern technology (Eskridge, French, Mc Thomas, 2012).

Applicable laws, regulations and policies affecting the NYPD financial and budgetary operations

Public sector finance budget is different from private sector finance budgeting in organizations. According to Mikesell, the reasons why public sectors engaged in public budgeting and finance is because *"they don't want to go to jail for misuse of resources that belong to the public or to their organization ---- they operate in the public trust and need to be able to control the use of public resources ----- they are using others people's money, and those people get mad when the money"* is not accounted for (2014, p. 1). For example, Police Commissioner Bernard Keri was a good commissioner however certain traits were deemed unethical by the public during his term of office such as corruption, and he was jailed for that purpose. Therefore, as a public servant, can't just act anyhow or use funds anyhow especially where tax payer's money is involved.

Also, Jacqueline Byers (Laureate Education, 2008c) stated that finance budgeting entails communication tools, strategic planning, financial document, and involvement of stakeholders input. In the NYPD, there is budgeting department that plans and document all NYPD finances, and the final version is reviewed by the current police commission before submitted to City Hall and the mayor of New York City for approval. This involves communication with the departments involved, and experts who plan the budget to come up with a financial document, and after approval a financial press is conducted for the audience or for all stakeholders to hear the financial budget.

In this case, the department fulfills the requirements by law to release financial analysis report to the public so that, they would be aware of what their tax payer's money is being used for. It is unknown if the NYPD has been a prey to miss-management however there have been government agencies that have been reported to have miss-used public funds negatively, and parties involved in the scandal were jailed.

Evaluation of the NYPD budget process and revenue sources Budget Cycle

According to Byers, the budget cycle involves: review of performance level, forecast needs of the growth and expansion of the organization; forecast costs, technologies, measuring and using traditional formulas to implement the budget plans. For the NYPD, each year, the finance budgeting unit made up of civilians and uniformed workers review and evaluate the performance of workers, accessing their input, and the resources used in the performance of their duties. They plan the budget to incorporate funds to be allotted to resources needed by the employees to work effectively to achieve the mission and goals of the department. Also each year computers and software's are updated to become abreast with modern technology. The planning team, plan in connection with short and long term goals, and what is currently going on in the department. They also plan what they intend to do for the fiscal year bearing in mind events and the calendar of the year. They also incorporate strategic planning as to how they are going to implement all these plans using revenue allotted from the Office of Comptroller. The financial officer gives the final stamp to the plans before it goes to the Police Commissioner for approval.

Forecasts

Mikesell stated that forecast deals with the future performance and evaluation of an organization (2014, p. 174). In the NYPD, we have short term and long term goals aligned with the vision, mission and goals of the police department. One financial planning for long term goal is for the department to renovate all the precincts within ten years. Another long term goal is for the officers to be good role models in fighting against terrorist and Islamic militants. With this in mind, the department is ready to increase wages based on performance evaluations for the employees.

Deficits

According to Mikesell deficits happens when the budget allotted to the department or government agencies is less than the organization intend to do in a fiscal year (2014, p. 135). In one instance, the police department had to negotiate with the unions during contracting to cut off provisional workers, and laid them off to balance the budget and finances during the term of Mayor Bloomberg. This happened because there was a huge deficit in the city coffers, and the unions wanted a raise therefore, it was a give and take issue which resulted in giving up provisional workers for permanent workers to have raises for three years. Although it was not fair for Provisionals to lose their job at permanent workers expenses, they were temporary workers, and are not required to take city exams, and were made aware that by law they could lose their jobs any time. Therefore, the law was applied to the situation, and the Provisionals lost their jobs. Permanent workers are entitle to a raise, and cannot be fired easily because they took the city exams, and have job security via contract binding agreement with the city and the unions. They have the support of the unions, and a binding contract stating that the department cannot just fire a permanent worker. The Provisionals had no support or contract backing their position, and don't belong to a union therefore it was easy to let them go.

One challenge faced in the long term goal of renovating the precincts is the fact that some precincts have the opportunity to utilize their renovated commands promptly while others have to wait for their turn, and this does not auger well in commands that are still waiting for the renovation. This places strains on precincts that are anticipating change causing stress and impatience. It is understandable that such commands are anxious however, the project would be done according to how the city releases funds. Normally the precincts close to major commercial areas are taken care off first, and then the non-busy commands.

The department cannot afford to hire contractors all over the station houses to complete the project in a short time because this may cause a deficit, therefore only a few contractors are hired, and they move from one command to the other. Also being that it would take years, it does not create deficit in the department coffers because the expenses are carried and added on to the next fiscal year's budget based on how many station houses the department envision to renovate in a year (Mikesell, 2014).

Stakeholders

Stakeholders in the NYPD are: the mayor, city hall officials, government agencies personnel's, police commissioner, deputy police commissioner, decision heads, members of benevolent associations, union delegates, lawyers, NYPD employees both civilians and uniform members, representatives, secretaries, researchers and the general public. According to Bryson (2011), stakeholders in an organization could create a unified meaning of ideas, goals and missions when each unit provides a representative or delegate to be presented, and inclusive in the strategic planning committee. Each representative would send back the message of decisions made for the organization, and the implementation procedure requirements to the rest of the stakeholders when the committee finishes planning for the organization. Also training and educative activities of what is supposed to be implemented for a unified goal would prepare stakeholders to enforce goals and aspirations of the organization. Also holding of forums and meetings among units and stakeholders would cause all involved in the organization to participate in unified ideas, and sharing would re-establish and enforce goals and missions of the organization. In order for implementation of strategic planning, a financial assessment must be in place to evaluate funds necessary for implementation of mission goals and visions (Bryson, 2011).

Enterprise Funds

Byers ((Laureate Education, 2008c) referred to enterprising as funds that a government agency charges on certain services to customers or the public. In the case of the Police Department, charges such as arrest, fines, tickets, summons and parking meter funds are received from the public to supplement the police department revenue. Previously, accident reports used to be charged ten dollars however, now, it is free to get a copy of a motor vehicle accident. However for finger printing in the police department, the charge has increased from $15 dollars to $25 dollars because of the high cost of the materials used for the finger printing systems. For example ink prices have soared high, and becoming very expensive, that is why the police department increased the price for finger printing.

Internal factors impacting successful strategic financial planning

Some internal factors that affect the development for a successful financial strategic plan is the fact that workers that work in the human resource units are made up of civilians, and sometimes there are conflicts between the civilian workers and the uniform employees. The uniform members deal and solve issues technically, and would want to apply that to the civilian operations however, civilian workers operate by code of ethics in human resources, and there is a clash on how to work in uniformism. For instance an officer placed on telephone operation unit would be professional not necessarily nice and friendly to complainants, and that is acceptable. According to human resource ethics, a phone operator must be nice, friendly, and courteous (EHow, n.d.). It is expensive to place an officer on telephone switchboard because technicality the officer is supposed to patrol the streets of New York City and is paid for such. The department pays less to hire a receptionist for the job. The officers would love to do the receptionist job because it is easy, and don't want to go on the street, however, that is not the job of an officer. So it is a conflict. The more officers stay to do clerical jobs, the more the city loses money because they are paid to patrol the streets of New York. Also, the department encourages officers that have disability or on restricted duties to retire because, it is waste of money because they are paid full salary to stay in the commands or to do clericals duties, whereas a civilian could do the same job for less pay. When officers retire due to disability reasons, they are not paid full salary, and so this helps the department restructure and adjust funds efficiently so that funds available could cover necessary police over-time and other expenses.

The NYPD's usage of cost-benefit analysis

The NYPD is funded by city funds, other categorical funds, state funds, federal C-D funds, other federal funding and intra city funding (The Council of the City of New York, 2013). The fiscal preliminary budget for the 2015 was 4.67 billion which reflects a modest "reduction of 1.6 percent or $79.7 million to its fiscal of 2014 adapted budget of $4.76 billion" (The Council of the City of New York, 2013). The deceased in non-city funds of $112 million accounts for the reduction of the funds allotted to the NYPD. Every year's funds may increase or decrease based on funds available to the different agencies by the City Comptroller who releases the funds to the various agencies.

According to Business Dictionary.com (n.d.), cost control includes 1) investigative procedures to detect variances of actual cost from budgeted costs; 2) it is a diagnostic procedure to ascertain the causes of variances, and 3) it is a corrective procedure to effect realignment between actual and budget costs. This point to the fact that in applying such principle to the budgetary of NYPD, there is a need to conduct an audit investigation of actual cost variance however the actual cost may be more or less. For instance, the 2014 budget for the NYPD was less than the budget for 2015. Auditors could determine the core of actual spending, and this may control poor spending estimated budget. The department may have to adjust between actual spending and estimated budgetary, and this would clarify and straighten out any poor miss-judgement or miss-calculations of the planned budget for the subsequent years. With this concept in mind, I believe that NYPD would be able to effectively calculate and differentiate between the exact spending from estimate to prevent poor revenue estimating mal-practices. With fair calculations, revenue would be spent with deliberations and appropriations. Also side funds received from the government, funds from fines could supplement the finances, and if not the department would have to consider exercising user fees principles to certain reports given freely to the public. Although it is free to make a report, accident fees use to apply for Police Accident Reports. In William Bill Bratton's term, this service fee has been cancelled. Although the fee was only $10 dollars, it helped purchase items such as cartridges and paper supply for processing. Since its stoppage, the department has not complained of paper or ink shortage, therefore, the department is well to do even though complainants don't pay for Accident Reports any more.

Dr. Henrietta Abeley Abbey

Evaluation of the NYPD's annual financial report

According to the Government Finance Officers Association (GFOA), it is a program opened to submissions *"from any type of government (general-purpose or special-purpose) at either the state or local level that makes available to the general public an operating budget documents in either an electronic (web site, CD) or hardcopy format, regardless of the length of the budget period (annual/biennial/triennial)"* (n.d.). Participants can send in a proposed or approved budget within ninety days of the date the budget was proposed (GFOA, n.d.). The GFOA awards the best agency with excellent achieve goal estimates. The report should meet expectations set forth by the GFOA. The GFOA awards the agency with the most excellent and quality documents of designed expenses.

Based on the criteria of the eligibility requirements, the NYPD 2014 budget report falls within the guidelines of GFOA. The report had heading followed by the table of contents. However it did not have an abstract to give a gist description of the substance although at a certain point in the report, the authors gave analysis of the budget report. From the heading, the Police Department was labeled in the commencement, and this is great because the reader or examiner could easily identify which city agency that the report is depicting. Also the heading stated that the expenses were for 2014, and it had date March 12, 2013 when the preliminary expenditure was drafted.

Also, from the report, the analysts started with an overview before the introduction however, the overview did not give detailed description of the department. It just listed Transit and Housing Police Department as add-ons to the organization. A full description of the various units in the department would have painted a clear picture of why the department uses a huge amount of revenue to support the organization. When the total units are not listed into the report due to the fact that the data must be condensed and concise, this means that the department is not giving a detailed description of the finances, and may not win the GFOA award. Listing all the units may give a broader understanding of why the department spends many funds to provide safety for the city. May be previous years such units were included, however every year is a new year, and the various units must be included in the overview report because it gives the reviewer a vivid understanding of equating the capacity and volume of the employees to the budget. Also a new examiner may not know about previous reports, and may not have time to dig into the past for such information. Therefore, the volume capacity of the department should have been included. Also a rough estimate of the total amount of employees listed could draw more meaning to the calculations of the various tables listed to give the report some kind of positive quality.

Furthermore, the report has previous spending dating back to 2011 (The Council of the City of New York, 2013). Also 2015 plans for the department were included (The Council of the City of New York, 2013). This gives the reader an excellent picture of how much was spent, balances, deficits and surplus of the subsequent years. Not only did the report provide tables and columns stating figures of spending but in words and sentences read explicit description of the table of expenses making the reader or examiner to have preference in understanding the report. If the report had included tables of figures without word/sentence description, a reviewer who is not mathematically inclining would have problems understanding just figures. Although not a research report, the idea and design is equivalent to Mixed Methods Approach because there were figures and vivid descriptive sentences to explain further details of the budget.

According to Northouse, an example of a budget outcome that results in the agency accomplishing goals such as the Police Department are: "hours on patrol, responses to call for assistance, crime investigation by category, number of arrests, police office present station to school children" (2016, p. 275). This means that in reporting a budget, such suggested details must be incorporated onto draft of the proposed budget. The 2014 Preliminary Budget for the NYPD stated crime classification and statistics on crimes in the schools but did not state all the Police Department Units. An accurate draft should have full details on spending, and crime statistics in the proposed budget plans. Also did the previous year budget accomplish the department's missions and goals? Which units achieved short or long term goals in the department with funds and resources offered? Also, although it did state some strategic plans in the report such as what the departments anticipate to offer in 2014, through 2015, it did not give vivid details, and did not report it in depths. Therefore based on the criteria of requirement, I would say the report is fair, however to win a competitive award suggested details are important.

The draft showed achieved spending goals in that both table and written statements explained spending goals. For instance the year of spending dates back to 2012, and stating the exact figures spent. For instance in 2012 the actual full-time salary for Uniform Members was stated as $1, 302,844, and in 2013 $1, 298, 70 was adopted, and the spending was "current modified" to $1,305,185; and in 2014 the statement read, January plan for 2014 was $1,305,185, and the difference between 2013-2014 was $6,484; all for full-time uniform services members (The Council of the City of New York, 2013). Therefore, in 2013, the drafted figures dropped but rose to an actual figures difference of $2341. This means that the budget went up. I also noticed that every year the new expenses go up, yet the budget did not include how the department made up for the raised difference.

Also, the budget plan meets revenue expectations as required by the GFOA because the Police Department documents stated actual spending and funds that it received from the government and its operations. It also dissected some spending figures of some units that the department uses to serve the public. For example it included spending on some units such as the IAB, Counter-Terrorism, Housing Bureau, Patrol Services, Criminal Justices, Special Operations, and Communications (The Council of the City of New York, 2013). It also stated the performance statistics, reimbursable over-time, and strategic plains budget from 2013 through 2016. This proves that the data had ample Statistic Analysis but an expert would want more details, and more information on the report. It is debatable that for the public a detailed report is not necessary however from an expert examiner point of view, or from a scholars perspective, there are loopholes in the report although it falls in line with the guidelines of the GFOA.

Assessment of the NYPD's overall financial condition

According to Williams, "productivity, or the lack of it, seems to be a widespread personal and organizational problem" (2015). Williams relates decline of personnel productivity to three key factors which are "work-life balance, workaholic and stress" (2015). This shows that sometimes, it is not in the best of interest that a worker be provided over-time. Each worker with his or her capability to work, therefore, the supervisors in the various civilian units would have to assess the various workers to determine who is capable of doing excess work. For the officers it is mandatory because each officer and the required arrests to process for the month. Although the officer's job is to deter crime, and it may appear emotional to arrest a citizen, by law, it is required that the officers maintain certain arrest figures statistics per month, and it is part of their rating in performance assessment. Also sometimes being workaholic does not mean the employee can perform best so, for the NYPD to have effective production from personnel's from the various work places, there should be constant evaluation and assessment of performance, and this could help supervisors assign extra work to workers that are capable of doing over-time. Sometimes officers could ask fellow officer to take an arrest when the assigned officer is too stressed out. When performance is addressed, productivity excels, and could help in planning finances and budgets the correct manner.

With the NYPD, some years the budget is high, and other times, the budget is low. Normally the estimated budget could be higher than the previous year however, with the aid of auditors that can improve. Auditors have the ability to cut cost to suite the department needs and resources. Most times the department have access to city auditors who are not affiliated with the department to conduct a thorough analysis of the financial budget, and that is why so far, there has not been any scandals involving the NYPD's fiscal financial budgeting reports. The credit goes to the effective leadership skills employed by commissioners elected. Even with Police Commissioner Bernard Keri, it was not the department's finances scandal but a personal bribery and corruption issue not related to finance and budgeting.

Conclusion

Thus the NYPD is a well-known establishment that have evolved from enforcing law and order, projecting ethical standards, and being abreast with computer age to more challenging missions to include fighting against terrorism. The financial analysis supports the fact that the department is still changing and improving for safety precautions which is the most substantial goal of the department. Based on the financial report provided, the department's agenda to provide excellent safety protection for New York City projects that the expenses of the department must be aligned with competitive demands of the millennium. Hence there is an alert that as the department continue to plan to effect and affect the general public with the law, and to protect New Yorkers and tourists, and the NYPD would plan strategically and profoundly in finance and budgeting to accomplish their aims and visions for the city of New York.

References

Bryson, J.M. (2011). *Strategic planning for public and nonprofit organizations: A guide to strengthening and sustaining organizational achievement (4th Ed.)*. San Francisco, CA: Jossey-Bass.

BusinessDictionary.com. (n.d.). Cost control. Retrieved from http://www.businessdictionary.com/definition/cost-control.html

Cali, M. (2010) NYPD paid nearly $1 billion to settle lawsuit. Retrieved from http://newyork.cbslocal.com/2010/10/14/nypd-paid-nearly-1-billion-to-settle-lawsuits/

Casey, J. P., & Seay, K. T. (2010). The role of the finance officer in strategic planning. *Government Finance Review, 26*(6), 28–36. Retrieved from the Walden Library databases

Ehow. (n.d.). Function of a receptionist. Retrieved from http://www.ehow.com/info_8573411_function-receptionist.html

Eskridge, R. D., French, P. E., & McThomas, M. (2012). The international city/county management association code of ethics. *Public Integrity, 14*(2), 127–150.

Retrieved from the Walden Library databases

Laureate Education (Producer). (2008c). *Introduction to finance and budget administration* [Video file]. Retrieved from https://class.waldenu.edu

Mikesell, J. L. (2014). *Fiscal administration: Analysis and applications for the public sector* (9th ed.). Boston, MA: Wadsworth.

Office of Financial Management. (n.d.). Comprehensive Annual Financial Report. Retrieved from **http://www.ofm.wa.gov/cafr/**

The Council of the City of New York. (2013). Hearing on the fiscal 2015 preliminary budgets & the fiscal 2014 preliminary mayor's management report: police department. Retrieved from http://council.nyc.gov/downloads/pdf/budget/2015/15/056%20Police%20Department.pdf

The New York City Police Department Official Website (n.d.). Retrieved from http://www.nyc.gov/html/nypd/html/careers/civilian_employment.shtml

Williams, R. (2015). The decline of personal productivity, and how to fix it. Retrieved from https://www.psychologytoday.com/blog/wired-success/201506/the-decline-personal-productivity-and-how-fix-it

The Language of Leadership:
The Statesmanship of Michael Bloomberg

Project completed on
October 17th, 2016

Abstract

This writing sample is about the analysis of former Mayor Michael Bloomberg's background and leadership skills that brought about his fame as a successful politician and a businessman.

Introduction

Leadership plays an important role in modern world because of the demand for leaders in the various systems of operations. According to Northouse, "leadership is a highly sought-after and highly valued commodity" (p. 1) due to advancement in society, and the need to look up to role models and leaders for inspiration, direction and for aspirations for future accomplishments. Leadership influences members, followers or workers, and inspire such entities to live up to expectation, for job satisfaction, motivation, and to excel. Leadership is inevitable, and it is generally apparent in organizations, establishments and institutions. One such leader whose attributes and tenets are so profound and outstanding is former Mayor Michael Bloomberg. I choose Bloomberg because he was a public servant who worked in government agencies and organizations, and he preached what he practices. His success and achievements in the financial areas are a plus to humanity and New York City as a whole.

Firstly I will introduce Bloomberg by talking about his autobiography, and fact that his educational experience played a role in his massive success in financial operations. Secondly, I would talk about his contribution to society, and to the populace in New York, the United States as a while including being an advocate for Gun control measures, and what he stands for globally. Thirdly would conduct leadership analysis of his behavior and language, and how he used leadership language to influence others, and the society at large. Fourthly would elaborate on recommending Bloomberg's as a father, transformational leader, public servant, and would include theory based recommendations for Bloomberg's improvement especially if he hopes to stand for president which he is debating on doing. I will also discuss the advantage and disadvantages that faces Bloomberg as a challenge for presidential candidate. I will also discuss and evaluate Bloomberg's behavior for sustainability Finally, I will conclude by summarizing the salient points and personal insights regarding Bloomberg as well as his impact on social change at the individual level, group level and society as a whole.

Bloomberg's biography

Former mayor Michael Bloomberg is a philanthropist, politician and a businessman. Bloomberg was born February 14th 1942 in Boston Massachusetts at St. Elizabeth Hospital to the parents of William Henry Bloomberg and Charlotte Rubens Bloomberg. Bloomberg's father was a book keeper and his mother was from New Jersey (Bio.com, n.d.). While growing up, he attended university at Johns Hopkins and Harvard. He specialized in Business Administration and received a master's degree in that field in 1966 (Bio.com, n.d.). He divorced his wife Susan Brown in 1973 whom he had two daughters, Emma Frissora and Georgina Bloomberg. From 2000 to now, he kept a low profile on intimacy with his domestic partner/girlfriend whom he is seriously involved in. During his term as mayor, his girlfriend Diana Taylor kept a low profile, and was not in the deem light as other mayoral wives as in the case of Mayor Bill De Blasio's wife Chirlane McCray involvement in women's movements.

Due to Bloomberg's quest for business, after achieving a degree in the business field, he started his first job in Wall Street with Salmon Brother, and worked hard and became partners with the company heads. He later bought the company and renamed it Bloomberg L.P in 1981 (Bio.com, n.d.). Bloomberg realized that his educational background assisted in the business field thereby allowing him to manipulate financially in the information age that revolutionized his business through secured data and stored consummation (Bio, n.d.). As the business progressed, he navigated to media business whereby he established 100 offices in the media world internationally, and that was when he geared his attention to establish himself as a philanthropist (Bio.com, n.d.). He became the 108th mayor of New York City in 2002. He served New York City as mayor for three terms.

Bloomberg's contribution to society and New York City

In 2002, he considered himself liberal Republican. He legalized same-sex marriage in New York City to decrease unfaithfulness and unhealthy relationships that cause illnesses such as HIV & Aids. He established a 311 telephone system that allowed New Yorkers to contact the city to report crimes and noncriminal incidents such as: trash issues, noise, animal curbing, smoking in public parks, and surroundings and/or issues which are city hazards or threats to society. He was re-elected in 2005 and 2009. In 2009, he campaigned for mayor a third term as an independent political party using 90 million USA dollars of his own personal money (Bio, n.d.).

It is worth noticing that when Bloomberg came into power, New York City had suffered a deadly blow of destruction being the World Trade Center Bombing which caused economic depression in New York City and in U.S. economy. Bloomberg was able to steering the finances of New York City into recovering from debt. During the 2012 financial reports for New York City, the mayoral management accountability report released that Bloomberg managed to accrue a surplus of 1.6 billion dollars with 72.7 billion budgets for 2012 (Pasanen, 2013). Here is a leader who applied business techniques to government finances and out of huge debts in 2002 New York City survived with a surplus in 2012. It takes a strong and intelligent personal such as Bloomberg to rebuild New York City, and another World Financial District.

Also, Bloomberg privatilized some of the government institutions, and using funds from taxes levied on property and sales taxes to fund education or elementary and high schools. In privatilizing some government schools, not only did it elevate the burden of government funds being used to rehabilitate such institutions but also saved the city revenue. Bloomberg also built a lot of affordable houses for low income breadwinners thereby creating shelter for New Yorkers who were living in private structures that were expensive. He also donated funds to cover shelters. Now the populace does not encounter homelessness people in the street as before due to funds being pumped into affordable housing and shelters for families in New York City.

On October 29th a tropical storm hit New York City. The storm caused floods in the streets, tunnels and subways cutting power in and around the city. It was estimated that the damage alone was over 68 billion USD in June 2012. About 286 people were killed due to the storm in the 7 countries affected. The unusual merge of the storm caused it to be nicknamed "Superstorm Sandy" by the media and organizations of the U.S. government. Initially, the storm started developing as a tropical wave from the Western Caribbean Sea. It then moved slowly toward Greater Antilles and then became a hurricane landing in Kingston Jamaica and to the Caribbean Sea. The storm moved to Cuba, then to the Bahamas and to northwest shores near Brigantine New Jersey the Northeast of Atlantic City which then affected New York City. The storm affected 24 States in the United States and Wall Street closed its doors during the Sandy Superstorm.

Some Corporations in New York City were displaced for weeks after the storm, and some employers and employees were relocated to temporary offices. Neighboring skyscrapers infrastructure and electrical systems that harbored Manhattan Financial Companies were also destroyed. Con Edison stated that 10 major buildings did not have power for several months and some were operating on emergency generators. 27 story office towers at 110 Wall Street near the Stock Exchange were badly damaged with floods. Phone and internet services hindered business activity when underground copper cables operated by Verizon the largest network provider were destroyed by the flood. By Mid-February 2013, Verizon said only 10% of its customers had little service.

Bloomberg, realizing that Superstorm Sandy was a wildcat threat to the restoration of New York recession, urged New Yorkers to vote for him so he could tackle this new threat of destruction that was able to erode New York City finances. Thus through thick and thin, Bloomberg was able to assure New Yorkers to stay calm, and lobbied for financial relief from the government as New York City was declared state of emergency crisis (YouTube, 2012). As the financial district was damaged badly Bloomberg knew that without strong analysis of the finances and help from the government, New York would plunge back into debt or recession. Thus with a strong and firm grip of the finances, Bloomberg was able to calm New Yorkers down, assisting those who lost homes, lost lives and property (YouTube, 2012). By the time Bloomberg was leaving office, there was a surplus even after the storm, and that was remarkable amazing and impressive of his skills as an abled leader.

Leadership Analysis

Bloomberg's leadership skills could be traced to two major leadership paradigms which are Transformational and Servant Leadership. According to Northouse (2016), Transformation Leadership could be defined as attention focus on "intrinsic motivation and follower development, which fits the needs of today's work groups, who want to be inspired and empowered to succeed in times of uncertainty (p.163). Under Bloomberg's leadership, a lot of businesses erupted in New York City. Organizations that planned migrating to other parts of the states and the world due to the 9/11 changed course, and remained in the city to rebuild the economy of New York City under Bloomberg's leadership.

Also Servant Leadership could be related to leaders in government agencies and organizations since most of the services are geared towards serving the public as a public sector organization (Chung, Chan, Kyle, & Petrick, 2010). Thus Bloomberg served New Yorkers through thick and thin. During the Sandy Superstorm, he held press meetings to educate New Yorkers on the updates of the storm. During the storm, he went to the shelter locations to help citizens who were displaced. He is one of the few mayors who spoke fluent Spanish (a second language), and did use it to communicate with the Spanish speaking people. His humility, demeanor, and tone of voice in reaching out to the populace, and to New Yorkers were influential. He neither raised his voice, nor got angry. He was rich and a mayor but understood the theory of servanthood and transformed New York City by fortifying the financial systems of the economy.

Bloomberg was ubiquitous, and punctual to every event. He frequently gave speeches and stories that resonate with the citizens. He opened the eyes of New Yorkers by showing through talk and body language ventures appropriate for the city, and those that are harmful to the city. His speech for a third term netted a pull thereby winning majority of New Yorkers vote after spending 90 million dollars for campaigning. Although majority wanted him as mayor for the third term, a few New Yorkers and other people from different parts of the world and state saw him as power drunk and poisonous. Thus during his third term he because so unpopular that one may wonder if he was the same person that brought New York out of recession, and re-organize Wall Street after the Sandy Storm? Also his refusal to negotiate and sign contracts with the unions concerning city workers expiration contracts for three or more years was questionable, and raised a lot of concerns. This is why he became so unpopular because the funds were there, there was a surplus, and yet he refused to negotiate with the union leaders for new contracts for city workers. City workers, and New Yorkers, reacted negatively to his unconcern for new contracts, and that tarnished his image despite his good works as mayor.

Another person who disapproved of Bloomberg's actions was Greenberg. In his article "Mayor Bloomberg's legacy: The good, the bad and the ugly", Greenberg stated that he disapproved of the Snapple contract that Bloomberg awarded a friend but Greenberg did not state the reasons why he disapproved the venture. Was it because Bloomberg was showing nepotism because he awarded the contract to a friend? The question is if you are a leader in Bloomberg's shoes, would you help a friend?

Furthermore, some New Yorkers were unhappy that some public schools were closed down to pave way for charter schools. Although privatalization saved cost, students whose schools were closed down had to be inconvenient in relocating to another school, and sometimes, the school was not in their district. The long commute and parent's frustration of parents finding transportation for their children through long commute made some of Bloomberg's ventures inconsiderate. This shows the give and take of the issues that Bloomberg had to face because, although he helped New York after 9/11, there were some who had to suffer because of certain actions taken by his administration. For instance Bloomberg and the teachers union were not able to agree on a contract and the city lost $450 million funds for students and children who depended on the state and federal funding for education (Goldman, 2013). That was a substantial amount of funds that Bloomberg and the teachers union let go to the detriment of students learning needs.

Thus Bloomberg started influencing New Yorkers especially in the first and second term of office however his third term of office was chaotic such as the failing to meet the deadline of state and federal funding of the $450. Bloomberg from onset was the leader that used personal stories and "meet the guru story" in influencing others (Settle, 2012). What happened during this third term in office? Was it better to have reigned for two terms and had great impact or for three terms, and tarnish the image and impact made? Why wouldn't Bloomberg sign the contracts with the city unions when there were funds available? Why did Bloomberg and the teachers union have to wait the last minute to negotiate on teachers' evaluation because last minutes are dangerous, and that was the exact thing that happened, the city lost that $450 million dollars funds at the expense of students learning needs.

According to Pierro, Raven, Amato & Belanger (2013), commitment to organization produces implications of great citizen's behavior, effective turnover rates and excellent performance. Bloomberg's first two terms were so effective that the citizenry reciprocated his service. New Yorkers were content the way he handled terrorist operations, and during his term, there was no terrorist operations or attack to New York City. Inspite of some negative sides, he was loved by the young, middle age and old folks. He served a multigenerational and multicultural populace, and most of the citizens approved and appreciate what he did for the city. He blended by using stories that pull and influence others, as well as used his power as mayor, as a rich man and a business man to bring transformation to New York City. Thus from Clawson (2012) three level of leadership, he started with self-leadership, then developing his skill and VABEs in affecting others, and in leading New York from anarchy into victory.

Leadership Recommendations

Despite the short comings of Mayor Bloomberg, he is highly recommended as a great leader. Although some people thought of him as power drunk due to his quest for three terms, he accomplished the goal of bring the city back to live because after 9/11, the city became a ghost town especially lower Manhattan where the bombing took place. Today, as an individual walks through the new World Trade Center, it is barely noticeable that the same place was a shamble in 2001.

Today, Bloomberg is a global business leader as stated by Clawson (2012). Clawson (2012) listed eight geographical identity categories of a global business leader which are: human, global region, nation, national region, city, neighborhood, family and individual (p. 187). I can identify with seven of the eight categories listed aligned with Bloomberg's global leadership. Bloomberg continue to work as a businessman globally, embracing all cultures, and he is still a philanthropist, and continues to lobby for legislatures to be passed for the American people. In order to be a global leader, an individual must be able to "respect the identities and affiliations of others" (Clawson, 2012, p. 187). As American faces controversies on gun plights, Bloomberg as usual invested $50 million to challenge the National Rifle Association (NRA) to enact laws that would protect the lives of innocent Americans being killed by arsenals. Bloomberg believes that money, power, education and the "meet the guru story" tenet can change the behavior of Americans who kill innocent lives (Settle, 2012). Thus his position as formal mayor and a lobbyist could help resolve issues pertaining to gun control?

Pierro, Raven, Amato & Belanger (2013) observed that previous studies revealed positive influence of change and charismatic leadership style impact commitment towards an organization. Pierro, Raven, Amato & Belanger (2013)stated that in line with interaction model, normally followers would willingly comply with soft bases of power rather than harsh stern authority, and that is the exact replicate of Bloomberg. He has a soft tone of voice, and character which he utilizes in commanding followers to comply to his command, and he wish to use that in addition to money to influence the NRA in enacting laws to protect the individuals from group gun assaults in the communities in America.

Bloomberg has overseer's experience, as deep self-awareness, and is culturally diverse due to serving New York City (Clawson, 2012). He is humble, has lifelong learning curiosity, very honest, has globally strategic and techniques in leadership (Clawson, 2012). He is patient, well spoken, a good negotiator, very human and all presence (Clawson, 2012). Also Simmons (2006) explained how storytelling is equivalent to culture keeper. As storytelling "are a vital force in molding the culture of "an organization, community and family, so was Bloomberg's leadership designed to help the communities, families and New Yorkers as a whole (Simmons, 2006). For instance, he built shelters and affordable houses for New Yorkers, and today, the city has only a few homeless people loitering the streets. When Bloomberg came into power, there were so many discrepancies regarding rent soaring high, and his answer was to build modern building homes for New Yorkers, with low income which prevented a lot of families sleeping in the streets.

Bloomberg would have been a fine president should he decide to run for president and should the American people vote for him. The only problem is that he is not married. He did not re-marry his domestic partner although they have lived for a long time. In this case, his domestic partner is common-law wife since they have lived for a long time. However with American values of first lady, would the people be ready to accept Bloomberg's domestic partner as first lady?

Furthermore, Greenberg (2014) explained how he was so unpopular with regards to stop and frisk, arrests and marijuana. Bloomberg believed in order and policies protecting the citizenry however he also believed that disobedience of the law must be punished so the law breaker may not repeat the same mistake again. This explains why New Yorkers with marijuana problems were arrested because the offenders were forming a habit of smoking in public which was health hazard to the public and nonsmokers. Stop and frisk was a big issue when Bill De Blasio inherited Bloomberg. Bloomberg made sure the officers were in the street, checking suspicious cars, and these helped prevented further terrorist attacks. Bill De Blasio discouraged stop and frisk, and marijuana possession, and currently New York has experienced two terrorist attacks to the detriment of tourists who want to travel to New York. Terrorist activities would limit tourists flowing to New York to boost the economy, and could reduce funds generated out of the tourist industry for infrastructure, and building of recreational amenities for citizens. Now with terrorist attacks surfacing, it would limit tourists who want to visit the New York City. Therefore, is it better for the police to continue with the stop and frisk, to arrest on marijuana smoking in public, and assigning special patrol of Islamic communities where terrorist attacks are suspected?

Again, Bloomberg was a mayor but he worked under Governor Andrew Cuomo. Bloomberg calls Cuomo the boss. He was submissive to Cuomo, and once stated on national television that Cuomo wanted them to go boat racing and attend a conference but he did not like it but Cuomo was the "boss" and he Bloomberg must do what Cuomo says. The manner in which he said it was very humble and submissive as described by Clawson (2012) and Simmons (2006) of how humble a leader should be. He was richer than Cuomo but then Cuomo was the boss, and he did not like certain rendezvous of the boss Bloomberg did not refuse rather he obliged because the boss commanded him to do so. He tried to live in harmony with authority, and with his administration that served with him. He encouraged his council speaker Christine Quinn to stand for election as mayor, and he financed her. He qualifies to lead the American people but the other question is that would Americans want a candidate who was a mayor, and an independent candidate? Initially Bloomberg was a democrat who was denied access to stand for mayor; therefore, he changed political affiliation to be a republican. During his third term of office, he changed affiliation to be an independent candidate, and it would be history if he wins for president as an independent candidate.

Conclusions

Some are born to lead while others learn the trait and tenets of leadership in institutions or organizations (Northouse, 2016). Bloomberg was both. He was born to lead, and he also used his learning skills in acquiring wealth, and re-structuring of New York City and its finances. However, politic is such that when an individual stays for a long time, that leader may become stale, and I think that is what happened to Bloomberg hence becoming so unpopular during the last years as mayor. Also, as a leader, it is possible not to please everybody. There are laws and ventures that may help others to the discomfort zone of others.

Thus from his experience in school, through his ability to make money with his company, to serving New York, Bloomberg has had a massive impact on the populace. He should be recommended for his continues fight and lobbying for laws to be enacted to protect individuals who lose their lives to violence. On the whole, I would rate Bloomberg 9 out of 10 in leadership style.

As an individual, I admire Bloomberg because of his humility, and the fact that he is very approachable. For instance during his third term campaign, some city staff members insulted him but he was humble and endure it to the end. Due to his style of approach in humbling himself to assist others, I love to do the same at work even when my co-workers hurt me, I still remember Bloomberg, and the ordeal he went through to serve New Yorkers, and I am prepared to do the same for people at work. Also he continues to help society and groups financially as he helped Christine Quinn. His business has extended globally in reaching out to society internationally. Therefore, voting the right person into government office is so important because then that person would be able to accomplish the goals and visions of the organization.

References

Bio. (n.d.). Michael Bloomberg. Retrieved from http://www.biography.com/people/michael-bloomberg-16466704

Chung, J. Y., Chan Su, J., Kyle, G. T., & Petrick, J. F. (2010). Servant leadership and procedural justice in the U.S. National Park Service: The Antecedents of job satisfaction. *Journal of Park & Recreation Administration,* 28(3), 1-15. Retrieved from http://web.a.ebscohost.com.ezp.waldenulibrary.org/ehost/pdfviewer/pdfviewer?sid=79c0d584-6bff-4b69-9b59-4d3b3b958719%40sessionmgr4007&vid=34&hid=4109

Clawson, J. G. (2012). *Level three leadership: Getting below the surface* (5th ed.). Upper Saddle River, NJ: Prentice Hall.

Goldman, H. (2013, January 18). NYC schools lose $450 million as teachers – Evaluation deal fails. Retrieved from http://www.bloomberg.com/news/articles/2013-01-17/nyc-schools-may-lose-450-million-as-evaluation-deadline-looms

Greenberg, J. (2014, March 9). Mayor Bloomberg's legacy: The good, the bad and the ugly. *Huffington Post.* Retrieved from http://www.huffingtonpost.com/jonathan-greenberg/mayor-bloombergs-legacy-t_b_4525526.html

Northouse, P. G. (2016). *Leadership: Theory and practice* (7th ed.). Thousand Oaks: CA: Sage Publications.

Pasanen, G. (2013, November 24). Analysis: The Bloomberg fiscal legacy. *Gotham Gazette.* Retrieved from http://www.gothamgazette.com/index.php/opinion/4739-the-bloomberg-fiscal-legacy

Peters, J. W. (2014, April 15). Bloomberg plans a $50 million challenge to the N.R.A. *New York Times*. Retrieved from http://www.nytimes.com/2014/04/16/us/bloomberg-plans-a-50-million-challenge-to-the-nra.html?_r=0

Pierro, A., Raven, B. H., Amato, C., & Bélanger, J. J. (2013). Bases of social power, leadership styles, and organizational commitment. *International Journal of Psychology,* 48(6), 1122–1134. DOI: 10.1080/00207594.2012.733398

Settle, B. (2012, March 8). 3 simple storytelling methods that can do your selling for you. *Copy Blogger*. Retrieved from http://www.copyblogger.com/marketing-with-stories/

Simmons, A. (2006). *The story factor: Inspiration, influence, and persuasion through the art of storytelling* (2nd ed.). Cambridge, MA: Perseus.

YouTube. (2012, October 30). Mayor Bloomberg updates New Yorkers on city's response to hurricane sandy. Retrieved from https://www.youtube.com/watch?v=mbYIANLOayw

References

The Making, Exploring, and Developing of
a Research Topic for a Qualitative Study.
The Importance and Meaning of Social Change
The Implication of Affecting Society Through Genre

Abstract

Research is essential to modern society. Here is an example of how to brainstorm, explore, and investigate a research topic to evolve into a quality masterpiece of literature or genre.

Introduction

Social change can be defined as "the transformation of culture and social institutions over time" (Study, n.d, p. 1). Change can be positive or negative. Social change can happen intentionally, unplanned, and could be controversial. Affecting society with the tenets and practical actions can stem up from learning. Sometimes individuals don't plan for social change but things happen such as wildcats, and that causes humans to change things around. For instance 9/11 was not planned however; out of the bombing were enacted Homeland Security, The Patriot Act and Security Administration (TSA) to ensure the safety of the Americans, and to prevent further bombing in the United States (Study, n.d.).

Social Change as a social issue

Also change involves researching about the topic and preparing for the outcome of the change. Out of research study could inform audiences about phenomena, directives, traits and advise as to how to live. Studies also warn audience about predicaments, and how to steer away from ailments. It is not enough just to perform research. Out of research, organizations and institutions are developed and formed to affect social change. For instance, when Kundert discovered her son's illness, she researched on it (Kundert, 2012). She made discoveries which she published. Next she formed an organization entitled Fighting Addiction It Takes Account (FAITH) to help people with drug problems recover from the illness (Kundert, 2012). Not only did Kundert realized that her son was not the only person with the illness but approximately five to seven years now, drug overdose had become common, and was spreading in Green County in Wisconsin (Kundert, 2012). Change transforms lives, makes societal environment a better place to live in and solves issues in the communities. Also through deliberate appropriateness of affecting society, researchers use trends and formats of planned procedures in successfully interacting with the audience to pinpoint transformation of phenomena (Kezar, 2014). The subject of change in a research can be in the forms of a moral, an idea, an insight, an advise, an invention, and a meme. Although change is needed, change can be positive or detriment of a community, society or the populace. Change means adapting to new things which could be unbearable or disadvantage to an individual. For instance increase taxes on the rich would benefit the poor who depend on welfare but a disadvantage to the rich and affluent who have to dispose of cash in paying for such taxes.

Learned topic on social change as a research problem

Research is conducting studies to explore, examine, describe and provide analysis of an issue. Out of the movies watched, I leaned that society embraces change. Change is a constant practice in life. Some changes may be to an advantage and some may be to a disadvantage. It becomes a problem when the issue is unsolvable, and causing deaths, and misfortunes. This then leads to investigation through studies or research, and the issue becomes a research problem opened for investigation, for answers, cures, and solution. A learned topic on social change as a research problem is the brawl between police officers and minority groups in New York City (Moore, Eisinger, Parascandola, Tracy, & Schapiro, 2014).

Description of a research gap in my study

The scholar of change videos were excerpts of professionality, and impressively designed to explicitly convey message of hope repairs and understanding. However there are different kinds of research problems in other disciplines that the videos did not cover such as issues involving economics and capitalism, social problems as homelessness, unsafe social movements, riots, and political contentions as in political science. As a learner, I am challenged and stirred up to effect change using my own experience to influence society hence choosing to discover grounds where the police officers and minority groups could get along without killings or shooting each other (Moore, Eisinger, Parascandola, Tracy, & Schapiro, 2014). The reason why I'm involved is because I work for New York City Police Department, and I serve the populace too. It is disheartening to listen to the news daily on mishaps or misfortunes of individuals, society and people in general regarding the brawl between minority groups and the officers. The question is that what can I do as a graduate student and a worker with the New York City Police Department to improve rapport between civilians and officers? The research gap in my study is that there has not been research on social programs such as talk host shows to discourse the mounted tension therefore; I would interview officers and civilians to see if such a program would help them solve their differences.

The gap that the study will address

The study would address social change in New York City. It would address the current training of officers as adequate in tackling first hand situations as in firearms. Also Freud (n.d.) stated that there are several reasons that trigger an individual's action. Thus the corporal state of the officer or civilian at the time of incident should be assessed, and such information released to the populace so that they can understand the mental state of an individual prior to shooting (Freud, n.d.). For instance, sometimes during police confrontation, both the officer or civilian could panic, and this may cause irrational shooting as described by Freud (n.d.).

From the gap, create a brief purpose statement that is aligned with the following research question:

What is the meaning of social change for Walden graduate students?

The purpose of this critical and structural functionalism theories study is to fill the gap in understanding the developmental state of society and culture of police officers and civilians in New York City, and prescribe an effective measurement in elevating tension between the two groups (Chaney & Robertson, 2015). For a Walden Student social change means exercising practical actions that would help a community or society to benefit from the action. For social change, I would create an organization to mentor police officers and civilians and their family that are victims of shooting. Also would mentor, have programs and counseling sections for any civilian and officer with racial problems against each other by providing educative and alternative measures in solving hatred rather than using violence. These programs would be recorded and telecasted for viewer's participation, information and compliance. Hopefully it would benefit society, and there would be a drastic change in the way the two groups interact. The programs would find alternatives of shooting; instead of killing why not shoot to disable and wound to heal rather than shoot to kill. These could be discussed in counseling sections.

The role of the researcher

The role of the researcher is to first examine other workers as in the case of us (Students) viewing the excerpts on scholar of change movies. As a graduate student getting ready to make an impact in society, studying others research through taking notes, coding and writing memos of other scholars prepares me in applying what I have learned from the classroom into practical exercise. I could also use other studies by citing and quoting to support my research, to backup an idea I need to elaborate on. Furthermore, Creswell (2014) explained that, "the inquirer is typically involved in a sustained and intensive experience with participants" (p. 187). This means that as a researcher, I would be involved in intensive rapport with participants to engage in discourse to contribute towards the study.

As a graduate student involved in research it is important to learn formatting, theories and conceptual framework of the study I have in mind (Ravitch & Carl, 2016). This prepares me as a researcher to effect social change using appropriate methodology and language that would be explicit to the audience. Also, it prepares me to have quality and solid evidence such as in Topper's excerpt in supporting my benefit for society (Topper, 2014). My role is to choose an appropriate site for the study, decide the activities that will happen at the site and during discussion, how to report the interview and lastly evaluate the gains of the audience from the study (Creswell, 2014).

An ethical issue that may arise out of the study is informal introduction. During introduction, would state the purpose of the study, the rights of the participants, and ask if it is okay to record and make notes. When a focus group discussion is conducted in the study, and recorded, it may give the chance of me as the researcher having appropriate excerpt to interpret data. This may cost money, and may be a disadvantage because snacks have to be served in the discussion premise, and possibly incentives may be given, and these actions have to come out of my own pocket. This may mean limiting the amount of people to be involved in the group discussion. Also the research would be two different groups: the officers and civilians. Some may have been victims of shootings. Thus I would need a moderator or a research assistant to intervene when the need arises. . As a worker with the Police Department, I may be lured into siding with the officers because I am an insider, and this make cause bias and errors in the study; hence the need for a research assistant to aid in maintaining neutrality, in order to prescribe the accurate antidote.

Data Sources of social change

The first movie excerpt by Benjamin Isaac was retrieved from Walden Data Base. The movie was shot in a home environment but unknown location; possibly a neighboring community in the United States. The length of the excerpt was 3 minutes. The movie was recorded privately for the scholar of change competition in 2014. The second movie by Jackie Kundert was retrieved from Walden Data Base. It was recorded in Green County, Monroe Wisconsin in 2012. The length of the excerpt was 2 minutes. The movie was recorded privately for the scholar of change competition. The third source was an audio phone recorder used for social change interview by Henrietta Abbey. The interview took place in the home of Henrietta Abbey in the Bronx of New York. The interviewee was in South Dakota. The length of the interview was approximately 17 minutes 18 seconds. The interview was recorded on a cell phone device, and later transcribed. The interview took place on October 14th 2016 at 1100 hours promptly. The fourth and last data source on social change was article by Yob & Brewer with no date stated. It was retrieved from Walden Data Base. The article is entitled, "Working toward the common good: an online university's perspective on social change". The article is about twenty-five pages.

Instrumentation of data

Video #1 was developed by Benjamin Isaac, and published in 2014. The participant group for the video was Isaac's children and friends. The audiences were Walden students, faculty, and staff members. It was used for Walden student scholar of change competition in a virtual environment. Isaac's excerpt is appropriate for children learners, educators, and virtual audience beyond Walden. Additional insight on how the characters performed and the outcome would be appreciated. The video was cut short due to time and limits. Therefore in publishing it on-line beyond Walden environment, for a larger audience, Isaac could show the outcome of the kids who were given special need characters what happened, and then summarizing of a sound and concrete results. The result in the excerpt was not so obvious. With extension of the length Isaac could prove it via the children's characters.

Video #2 was developed by Jackie Kundert, and was published in 2012. The excerpt was used for Walden student scholar of change competition virtual environment. Previously, the excerpt was used in a competition, and the participants were people were people who were going through the same experience as Kundert. Kundert excerpt is appropriate especially for people and family experiencing drug addict problems. A larger audience on-line would love to learn how a problem turned into igniting of an organization and blessing others. I am not sure Kuhnert's son died. The video is unclear about that. The other woman at the cemetery was not Kundert therefore more insights needed to clarify whether it was Kuhnert's son that died or the other woman's child that died.

Excerpt #3 was an audio recording developed by Henrietta Abbey, and published in October 2016. An audio recording was used for a research assignment on social change which involved an interview. Abbey's audio recording was typically for an assignment, and the interviewee is entitled to a transcript as well as the professor. Participants in the recording was the interviewer (Abbey) and the Interviewee who responded by phone from South Dakota. The interviewer a current student of Walden, and the interviewee an alumni of Walden graduated 2016. Abbey could place the transcript on sharing document for fellow students and classmates to view and share experience and insights. In modification, Abbey could include video recording that is if the interviewee's phone and Abbey's phone had video phone recorder. The interview could be shorter for approximately ten to twelve minutes.

The fourth instrumental data applied that talked about social change was the article by Yob & Brewer, no date. It is unknown when the article was published. The article was developed by the authors Yob & Brewer. The article was meant for audiences that appreciate and are pro on social change. Students from natural environment or virtual surrounding could benefit from the article due to the fact that it talks about social change. It embraces all disciplines. One disadvantage about Yob & Brewer's article is the fact that it is unknown when the article was published. It would be difficult in relating it to a specific era, and drawing symbolic meanings related to the era, and how appropriately relevant it was in that era. Also virtual learning environment is known to be the information age era however a specific date would give more insight to events happening and surrounding the prompt for the article.

Data Analysis

Thus from all four data sources, one theme that runs through the videos, audio and article is social change. Social change is a broad topic. Each source, and the topics or disciplines that erupted from the sources' for instance Isaac in video #1 used education to enlighten the audience on social change regarding special education needs children. Kundert was a nurse, and she used that field in researching on drugs, and drug addiction. Kundert also found social organization that helped people with drug addiction. She expanded from her discipline nursing into social sciences or social work since her organization FAITH which has to do with serving people which is aligned with nursing. Abbey's interview was on social change, and the interviewee used his field of studies and his dissertation as an example of social change. His dissertation was on obesity, and how income could affect an individual's health which could cause obesity. According to the interviewee (2016), learning is another thing but using education to teach others what you have learned is what social change is about.

Furthermore, all four data sources could be categorized as: video #1 social change in education; video # 2 social changes in science, and social work; audio #1 social change in public health (epidemiology), article #1, social change in virtual learning environment.

Coding of data

1st Cycle	"That's why I am attempting to effect social change with the help of few very special friends of mine" (Isaac, 2014, p.1). "As a result Skeeter, the DJ, was voiced by Ian and Connor two children with autism" (Isaac, 2014, p. 2) "I started an organization called FAITH which stands for fighting addiction it takes account. And I believe it takes help not only from the addict, but also their family as well as a community"(Kundert, 2012, p. 1). "For me learning without impacting others and community is not good, I believe social change starts when you impact your community and society with what you have learned, that is why I instructed a group of people from my church on my study on obesity, and the fact that your income may determines an individual health life style" (Interviewee, 2016)

2nd Cycle	Education
	Friendship
	Community
	Social Change
	Learning to impact others
	Doing something with your learning skills
Themes	Social Change
	Community
	Learning
	Initiative
	Affecting society
	Having impact on community
	Family involvement
	Awareness

Chart

Trustworthiness

According to Shento (2004), trustworthiness ensures rigor in the study. Researchers satisfy their quest for knowledge and convey knowledge by addressing credibility, providing detail context of fieldwork for readers to decide the prevailing environment, and it's relevant to other setting, and whether it is applicable (Shento, 2004). Also Shento (2004) explained that when researcher's strife to enable future investigation, a repeat of the study is possible, and also researchers must demonstrate that the findings emerged from data, and not so much about the researcher's predisposition.

Thus from the four data collections the most common themes that surfaced were: social change; research; affecting the community; bring awareness to the populace or audience; taking initiative and learning. From Isaac's data, the themes were more of learning, education, social change, family and community. From Kundert's excerpt, the themes were different although some overlapped with Isaac's themes, the audio interview and the data from Walden Data Base. Kundert's themes were also community, family, awareness, education, death, and the consequences of drug addiction. The audio interview themes were, education, social change, interacting, and affecting society. The website data was about social change, education, the importance of virtual learning and virtual learning culture. Thus Kundert's theme of death was different from all the data collected. The data from Walden Data Base website's theme on virtual learning culture was also different from all the themes from the other data collection.

The results of the study on social change is believable a possible results from all four data collected. For instance Kundert effected positive change by establishing FAITH organization to save lives and to transform lives. The interviewee (2016) interviewed stated that there is no point in learning, and not bringing knowledge to others to encourage a change in life style. Thus the degree to which the results of the interviewee changed his church community by transferring school knowledge caused fellow church members to upgrade their learning for better jobs to afford a life style that may prevent obesity. One learning student can effect change by affecting the populace and the communities in triggering more learning and social change.

Thus from Isaac's movie, I leaned that people with special needs cannot be defined by their illness but through their characters. Thus through Isaac's research assumptions on special needs are proven to be the opposite. Rather children with special needs do perform excellently in school (Isaac, 2014). Thus the audience can count on the research to strife to enable future investigation by repeating the study (Shento, 2004). Thus as a student, I am learning about social change, so I could also affect others through an invention or through dissertation.

The themes from all four data source relate to social change although from different perspective. Therefore I can conclude all four sources are relevant in effecting social change. These four data sources could be references to further studies related to social change.

Summary

For me as a Walden graduate student, social change means doing something to change people's lives, bringing light and knowledge to someone, and making a great impact on others. As the interviewee (2016) stated, there is no point in keeping what you've learned when there are other people to receive the knowledge and that could change the life style of the individual for a good course. This reminds me of the smile on a child's face when given a cookie or candy. I think the same thing would happen, a smile, a relief or an impact on a life for quality social life is a blessing.

If there is any change in my understanding of social change it is more depths and quest to do something that would have positive impact on somebody. Not for fame but a reward of gratitude that I changed an audience understanding or perspective of a notion. I prefer Thomas, MCGarty & Mavor (2009) article because the authors examined the interaction of agents in producing combined massive impacts which are better than separate efforts. Thus with fellow students, I am learning to be an agent to impact others not as a separate entity but with support of my school Walden and faculty members we together net great effects on society.

References

Abbey, H. (2016). *Interview on social change* [Audio file]. Retrieved from unpublished manuscript, Walden University

Chaney, C., & Robertson, R. (2015). Armed and dangerous? An examination of fatal shootings of unarmed black people by police. *Journal of Pan African Studies*, 8(4), 45-78. Retrieved from http://web.b.ebscohost.com.ezp.waldenulibrary.org/ehost/pdfviewer/pdfviewer?sid=d4ede60c-57f8-4c65-9e4f-bafc1a7f3f74%40sessionmgr105&vid=4&hid=129

Creswell, J.W. (2014) *Research Design: qualitative, quantitative, and mixed method approaches (4th ed.)*. Thousand Oaks, CA: Sage Publication.

Freud, S. (n.d.). The neuro – psychoses of defense. Retrieved from https://books.google.com/books?hl=en&lr=&id=sn1-CgAAQBAJ&oi=fnd&pg=PP5&dq=sigmund+freud+1856+-+1939+neurological+state&ots=FBngYxpWoa&sig=aXdjXMPLaYg-a5_fYvi4w5asKN0#v=onepage&q&f=false

Isaac, B. (2014). *Benjamin Isaac, EdD student, inspiring children with special needs* [Video file]. Retrieved from Walden Data Base.

Kezar, A. (2014). Higher education change and social networks: A review of the research. *Journal of Higher Education, 85*(1), 91–125. Retrieved from Walden Data Base.

Kundert, J. (2012). *Battling drug addiction in the heartland.* [Video file]. Retrieved from Walden Data Base.

Moore, T., Eisinger, D. W., Parascandola, R., Tracy, T., & Schapiro, R. (2014, December 21). Two NYPD officers 'assassinated' while sitting in a patrol car in Brooklyn by gunman who boasted on Instagram about revenge killing cops (Graphic Images). *Daily News*. Retrieved from http://www.nydailynews.com/new-york/nyc-crime/cops-shot-brooklyn-sources-article-1.2051941

Ravitch, S. M., & Carl, N. M. (2016). *Qualitative research: Bridging the conceptual, theoretical, and methodological*. Thousand Oaks, CA: Sage Publications.

Shento, A. K. (2004). Strategies for ensuring trustworthiness in qualitative research projects. Education for Information, 22(2), 63-75. Retrieved from Walden Data Base.

Study. (n.d.). What is social change? – Forms & definition. Retrieved from http://study.com/academy/lesson/what-is-social-change-forms-definition-quiz.html

Thomas, E.F., MCGarty, C., & Mavor, K.I. (2009). Transforming "Apathy into movement": The role of prosocial emotions in motivation action for social change. *Personality & Social Psychology Review*, 13(4), 310-333. Doi: 10.1177/1088868309343290

Topper, C. (2014). *Christine Topper, PhD student, bringing the natural world to Hong Kong.* [Video file]. Retrieved from Walden Data Base.

Yob, I., & Brewer, P. (n.d.). Working toward the common good: An online university's perspective on social change, 1-25 Retrieved from https://class.waldenu.edu/bbcswebdav/institution/USW1/201710_27/XX_RSCH/RSCH_8310/readings/USW1_RSCH_8310_Yob_workingTowardTheCommonGoodArticle.pdf

www.ingramcontent.com/pod-product-compliance
Lightning Source LLC
Chambersburg PA
CBHW071032080526
44587CB00015B/2587